*Taking My Doggerel
for a Walk*

# Taking My Doggerel for a Walk

*A Miscellany of Verses, Limericks, Odes and the Like*

Jenny Caro

Copyright © 2018 Jenny Caro

The moral right of the author has been asserted.

Apart from any fair dealing for the purposes of research or private study, or criticism or review, as permitted under the Copyright, Designs and Patents Act 1988, this publication may only be reproduced, stored or transmitted, in any form or by any means, with the prior permission in writing of the publishers, or in the case of reprographic reproduction in accordance with the terms of licences issued by the Copyright Licensing Agency. Enquiries concerning reproduction outside those terms should be sent to the publishers.

Matador
9 Priory Business Park,
Wistow Road, Kibworth Beauchamp,
Leicestershire. LE8 0RX
Tel: 0116 279 2299
Email: books@troubador.co.uk
Web: www.troubador.co.uk/matador
Twitter: @matadorbooks

ISBN 978 1789015 683

British Library Cataloguing in Publication Data.
A catalogue record for this book is available from the British Library.

Printed and bound in Great Britain by 4edge Limited
Typeset in 11pt Adobe Garamond Pro by Troubador Publishing Ltd, Leicester, UK

Matador is an imprint of Troubador Publishing Ltd

Dedicated to all the canine and feline friends who have given me such joy during my life:

Tim, Snowy, Lil, Lucy, Mara, Etty, Mimee,
Bitha, Tippee-Mowgli, Maisy, Fuzzy,
Nala, Sylvie, Angie, Molly,
and George the Giant Cat.

# Contents

| | |
|---|---:|
| My Doggerel | 1 |
| The Welcome | 2 |
| Pigeon Post | 6 |
| The Golden Hinde | 7 |
| Two Bad Buses! | 10 |
| The Wedding | 12 |
| American Horrors | 15 |
| This Week's Bargain Offer | 16 |
| Life's Journey Home | 19 |
| Frankie – A Cautionary Tale | 21 |
| The Old Wisdom | 26 |
| Lost Partner | 27 |
| Close Encounters of the Household Kind | |
|    Part I: An Unwanted Visitor | 29 |
| Close Encounters of the Household Kind | |
|    Part II: Suddenly, Last Summer | 31 |
| Comfort | 33 |
| What a Blow! | 35 |
| Mr Gloomy | 38 |
| A Modern Biblical Tale | 41 |
| The Training Course | 43 |
| A Poetic Quandary | 48 |
| Lower Watha | 50 |
| Out for a Coffee etc | 53 |

| | |
|---|---:|
| The Humongous Supper | 54 |
| Posh Poetic Footie | 56 |
| Signora Brava | 57 |
| Spring Flowers at War | 59 |
| Detritus | 63 |
| Holiday Rap | 64 |
| Corn Circles | 66 |
| The Pillage of London | 67 |

# *Introduction*

You may think this question's perverse;
Does 'doggerel' mean barking in verse?
Oh no! I reply.
It's a fun way to try
Making poems or rhymes sound much worse.

For those readers who have not encountered the term **'doggerel'** before, it is poetry that is fairly simple in its structure, sometimes rhymed and sometimes not, and often rough-hewn or nonsensical in its content. It works well for burlesque or comic effect. It has a long history in English literature, having been used in Anglo-Saxon riddles and in wider literary works since at least 1630. There is a long tradition of more modern and very clever nonsense verse in English, with writers of great stature like Lewis Carroll and Ogden Nash.

The doggerel in this volume is only one element out of a whole variety of poetic outpourings – mainly amusing, some regular in rhythm and rhyme, some free verse, some cautionary tales and some serious writings – all in all, a real 'doggerel's breakfast' full of entertainment – enjoy!

# *My Doggerel*

My Doggerel is my best friend. He's been with me for years.
I love his shaggy, baggy coat and silly-billy ears.
He can be temperamental and not play the doggerel game.
I change his mind by telling him he'll never achieve great fame.
This usually does the trick and he'll produce a rhyme
That's funny and original and he'll let me call it mine.
And so, dear Reader, wonder not for whom this book to thank.
Just remember that without him all the pages would be blank!

# The Welcome

Come on in, my lovely!
So pleased to see you here.
Been looking forward for an age
To seeing you, my dear.

Here, let me take your overcoat
And that delightful hat.
I'd better put it somewhere safe
Or it'll end up flat.

Now make yourself at home, my dear.
Just treat this as your own.
It's only small, but cosy like
Just right for me alone.

Come and sit down here, my dear
In the best armchair.
You're by the fire and toasty warm.
I always sit right there.

I'll go and put the kettle on.
A lovely cup of tea
Will warm you up and we can chat
As happily as can be.

Now would you like a biscuit
Or a slice of seedy cake?
Don't want to boast but it's the best
Of all the things I make.

Did you want to 'you know what'?
Powder your nose, let's say.
I'll show you where it is, my dear,
You'll never find the way.

Ah, there you are. Another cup?
There's plenty in the pot
We'd better have it now, my dear,
While it's still nice and hot.

I'd better draw the curtains too.
The daylight's fading fast.
The nights are drawing in so soon.
The summers never last.

I'm sure you've got a lot of news
But just hold on, my dear.
I've saved up lots of gossip
Which I know you'll want to hear.

Well, did you know that that young lad
Who lives across the way,
Has made it known that he's 'come out'?
He's been a closet gay!

And what about old Daniel Brown;
Did you hear what he did?
He poisoned all the pigeons!
No – it's true. He really did.

And his old dad – you know, old Bill –
He's gone a bit doolally.
They found him in the dead of night
Asleep down some dark alley.

Such goings-on in this small place
Just in the last few days.
Enough to give us all the creeps
I'm well and truly fazed.

Why are you getting up, my dear?
Are you not comfy there?
Would you like another cushion?
Or you can have my chair.

Time to go? No, surely not.
You've only just got here,
And you've been very quiet today.
You've not said much, my dear.

Well, I must say I've so enjoyed
Your company today.
We've had a lovely chat, my dear.
You sure that you can't stay?

Well, cheerio and don't forget
When you need a listening ear.
I'm the one to come to
And you're always welcome here!

## *Pigeon Post*

I'm sitting collapsed on this garden post,
Composing a plea to the folk I love most.

My compass has broken. I truly am lost.
I need some assistance – I'm tired and storm-tossed.

No stars out tonight to give me a clue
On which direction to fly back to you.

I'm dreaming so sadly of my little loft
Where, warm and contented, I slumbered so oft.

I can picture your faces, bewildered, disturbed,
Fretting over the loss of your best racing bird.

I pray that, come morning, my skills will come back,
That sleep will restore me, no strength will I lack.

I'll remember my training and, straight as a die,
I hope I'll head homeward as the crows fly.

# *The Golden Hinde*

You could have knocked me down with a feather
A couple of weeks ago.
I still can't believe what happened.
It was so surreal, you know.

I was sitting outside of a cafe
With the *Golden Hinde* by my side.
That wonderful historic sailing ship
That was Francis Drake's joy and pride.

There were plenty of crowds all around her,
Admiring her beauty and grace,
When all of a sudden, a deathly hush
Descended upon that place.

The air around us grew murky.
A shadow appeared round the craft.
Then a shout was heard in that silence:
"Cast off fore and aft!"

We watched in open-mouthed wonder,
As her mooring ropes broke free.
Then, with many loud creakings and groanings,
Her great sails unfurled, flying free.

Her anchor rose from the waters
Of St Mary O's Dock where she lay.
Her sails filled with air, her prow rose up high,
She shuddered and then was away!

Free of her concrete cradle
Where many a year she had lain.
The victim of tourists' attentions
Whose ignorance caused her pain.

None of them gave her full credit
For circling the globe long ago.
In the days of swashing and buckling,
A bottle of rum – yo-ho-ho!

But now she's escaped, been reborn,
Come alive and ready to flee.
She breasted the tide of old father Thames
And danced on his waters with glee.

The silence then broke, and the crowd who had
    gaped
Now raised up their voices and cheered.
They sang *Merrie England* and threw up their caps
At the sight that so wondrous appeared.

Twelve guns spoke in a great cannonade,
Her pennants all waving free.
A shadowy figure stood at her wheel
In doublet and cape – was it he?

For borne on the wind as she sped fast away
Came a ghostly voice – was it Drake?
"I'm off to circle the world once again
For England and dear Bess's sake."

## *Two Bad Buses!*

The omnibus gave a sudden lurch
Just as we passed the big parish church.

A chorus of groans and half-shouts rose up:
What the heck's going on to so sharply pull up?

Did that lorry in front with the massive great load
Decide to pull out in the midst of the road?

Or was it that cabbie who raced up ahead
Like an F1 driver risen late from his bed?

Or did a pedestrian walk like a jay,
Risking his life to live one more day?

No! Nothing like that. The cause was surreal:
Our driver had fallen asleep at the wheel!

There once was a red London bus
Which was racing along with no fuss.
But a lurch to the right
To the passengers' fright
Caused a great deal of people to cuss.

The folks who were sitting on board
Fell forward with cries of "Oh Lord!"
There were shouts of alarm,
And "I've broken my arm!"
And most of them had been floored.

Emergency services came
To deal with the halt and the lame.
London Transport came too,
With a portable loo,
Saying, "Relief is the name of the game!"

# The Wedding

"Wedding? What wedding?" the young maiden cried.
"Your wedding," her nobleman father replied.
"But, Father, I mean, I am only fourteen;
So little of life and the world have I seen."

"Silence, my daughter – you are old enough
For your father to find a protector quite tough
To safeguard your honour. And keep you in style,
So stop all this nonsense and give me a smile."

"But who must I marry? I know of no man
I could love as only a woman can!"
"Why, I have selected a rich and bold knight
Sir Boris of Johnson, of ancient birthright.

"With pots of good sovereigns and plenty of land,
And royal connections. He'll give me a hand
In raising my status. To court I shall go
And be as a friend to our sovereign, you know."

"Oh no, dearest Father, he's old and he's fat!
You surely couldn't condemn me to that?!"
"Condemn you? What nonsense you young women speak.
Now do as I say. Be compliant and meek."

And so the days passed and the wedding drew near.
The young maiden sickened from worry and fear.
No morsel could tempt her, no drink passed her lips
She became like a beanstalk – no bust and no hips.

Her complexion was wan and her body so weak
She looked hardly mortal. She barely could speak.
Her tears never ceased – oh, how she would weep!
She was even found sobbing as she lay asleep.

On the eve of the nuptials, Sir Boris came late
To meet the girl's father and just celebrate.
They drank to the future with many a draught
Of the Rhenish sweet wine. Oh, how the pair laughed!

The wedding began – a veil still in place
To hide maiden blushes of the bride's face.
The vows and the prayers completed with pride.
The rings were exchanged and the knot firmly tied.

Then came the moment Sir Boris did rise
To lift up the veil from his young, tender prize.
But oh, what a shattering blow for this Knight
For now he beheld a most sickening sight.

The maiden he'd married – a juicy young prize –
Had a face like a Gorgon and murderous eyes.
She turned to her husband, and with a foul stare
Turned him to stone. He fell dead and lay there.

The bride turned and fled after cursing the scene.
She fled far away and was never more seen.
Her father, dumbfounded, his dreams lost and gone,
Was evermore haunted by what he'd done wrong.

Ne'er was there such sorrow, such torrents of woe.
A wedding of misfits – how else could it go?
All fathers take heed – make a vow, say amen
To ne'er wed your daughters to grisly old men.

# American Horrors

*She:*
There once was a Homecoming Queen
The worst one I ever have seen.
Obese and ill dressed
In gold trainers and vest,
And a gown coloured poisonous green.

*He:*
There once was a Homecoming King
Dressed as Siegfried from Wagner's *Ring*.
His tights were quite handy
To highlight his bandy
Two legs, which were thinner than string.

# This Week's Bargain Offer

When I got the parcel home
And freed it from its box,
I was lost for words at the size of it.
It blew off both my socks!

Looked at from every angle,
No one side was made straight.
There were knobs and springs and sliding
  things
And many a figure eight.

The man in the shop had told me
It was this week's bargain deal.
Two quid for a mystery appliance,
Really quite a steal!

I'd had to hire a flatbed truck
To get the monster home.
It weren't just the gizmo was supersize,
The instructions a foot-high tome!

"Blow that for a game of soldiers."
Chucking the tome in a ditch.
"I'm going to start off right away,"
I said. "Now, where's the on/off switch?"

I pushed it over and pushed it round,
But no on/off switch could be found.
I pressed some knobs, boinged a few springs
And slid every sliding thing around.

I struggled to make the thing go,
And it wasn't till Fred came around.
He tried all the things that I had tried.
No luck, but in turning it round,

Fred spied a very small notice
Stuck in a half-hidden groove:
*Press here for 3 and a half times*
*If you want this appliance to move.*

Fred pressed it; I pressed it,
Three and a half times as per.
The blessed thing just sat there sulking,
Not going anywhere – grrrr!

In the long time-honoured fashion
When everything's going awry,
Fred and I made a brew in the teapot;
The cup that cheers – oh aye.

We both sat and stared at the monster,
But as Fred gave a very loud cough,
The whole darned caboodle shook violently
And *whoosh* – it simply took off.

It flew round the kitchen, demented.
And dodging as best as we might,
Fred and I pulled open the kitchen door
And let the thing into the night.

Our relief! I just can't describe it.
We both sat in armchairs and dozed.
Then had a good laugh in the morning
As the locals discussed UFO's.

# *Life's Journey Home*

I can't believe that my starting step
Was so very long ago.
Yet now my journey's almost done.
Just a little way to go.

I came upon this goodly earth
Into a crib of love.
Mother and Father each of them
As kindly as a dove.

Nurtured from the very first
In warm and tender ways.
Guided and cherished through the years
Safely through life's days.

I grew and felt the mix of life;
The pleasure and the pain.
I too fulfilled my purpose
And gave life to newborn – twain.

I loved both daughters with all my heart;
In turn, their offspring too.
I lost their father from this earth;
The winter of life followed through.

And now upon the brink I stand,
For once all on my own.
I wait to know the chosen hour
When I will journey home.

# *Frankie –*
# *A Cautionary Tale*

That green and crazy summer
When Frankie was a lad,
A wild and wilful boy he was,
Who loved the mad and bad.

His head was full of myths and dreams.
He wove some stories grand
Where he was always hero,
A bright sword in his hand.

His summer hols were nearly done
And school was looming fast.
He yearned to do a valiant thing
Before the hols were past.

His mother Jane had done her best
To make the summer fun,
With shopping trips and painting sheds
And reading in the sun.

But none of these were Frankie's choice.
They bored him stiff and failed
To galvanise his fertile mind
Where knights of old prevailed.

"I'm bored to tears," said Frankie.
"(Not that I'd ever cry.)
I have to go adventuring
Before school comes on by."

So one fine night when all was quiet,
He ventured from his room.
He crept downstairs without a sound
And grabbed a household broom.

The front door opened with a creak.
He listened, but no sound.
He shut it quietly, bit by bit,
And then he turned around.

He crept across the garden.
He didn't make a sound.
Then ran and ran till breath was gone.
He stopped and looked around.

The warm night air and crescent moon
Were heaven to his eyes.
It was the perfect night for him
To start his enterprise.

He loved the dark, he loved the woods.
He heard the owls shriek loud.
Not one whit scared was little Frank;
*I'm brave*, he thought, *and proud.*

*I'm going to do a mighty deed
Of valour, strength and fame.
I'll be renowned throughout the land
And all will know my name.*

He stepped out boldly in the dark
And waved his broom about.
But when it caught in a bramble hedge
He couldn't get it out.

He shrugged and thought, *I don't need that.
No hero needs a prop.*
His next step didn't take him far:
In deep mud he did drop.

He wriggled to free up his feet
And lost his shoes instead.
*Oh well*, he thought, *"no matter.*
*On tiptoes I can tread."*

He took one step; he turned and then
He gave a dreadful yell!
He'd trodden on a hedgehog.
His tootsies hurt like hell.

He hopped about to quell the pain.
It just grew more intense.
He turned around to find the path
And ran into a fence.

That poor young lad had lost his dreams.
He whispered, "Oh, poor me."
Perhaps adventures weren't the joy
They were cracked up to be.

"What shall I do, where shall I go?
I'm lost! Will no one come?"
And then he heard a far-off shout;
It was his lovely mum!

He called her name incessantly
Until she reached his side.
He clasped her tight in that dark night
With all his might and cried.

Mum took him home and cleaned him up
With many a loving hug.
Bandaged his feet and soothed his soul
With cocoa in a mug.

No great recriminations,
For he was alive, not dead.
She took her boy back home again
And tucked him up in bed.

Young Frank had learned his lesson.
When you are young and roam
It brings no joy, and for a boy
There's no place like home.

## *The Old Wisdom*

Home is where the heart is.
Home's the sweetest place.
Home is where my slippers live,
Where smiles a well-loved face.

Home is a safe harbour
From storms and stormy seas.
Take me home, sweet chariot.
I need to find home's peace.

You may stray forty leagues away
Searching for rainbow's end,
But heart's greatest joy is just to find
Home's round the very next bend.

## Lost Partner

Oh, where has that man gone
Who once made my heart flutter?
That man, I fear, is hardly here;
He's spooning with his putter.

No more do we speak tender words
Of love and lasting passion.
He prowls the specialist sports shops
In search of golfing fashion.

It's many years since his best friend
Suggested a trial round,
And ever since that man's obsessed.
Nirvana he has found!

He's spending hours on practice shots.
"My grip's not right," he moans,
"And my backswing is quite shocking.
I fear I've brittle bones."

"Come here, my dear," I sweetly say;
"I'll cure your grip and swing.
I'd like to practise gripping you
And your dear neck to wring.

"I'd like to lay you on the ground
And jump upon your bones.
It may not cure your backswing
But I'll love to hear your moans."

All right for him, this golfing lark,
But what's in it for me?
A golfing widow half my life;
I'm only forty-three!

Our daily life is one long grind
Of bunkers, holes and putts.
It's just not bearable no more.
I feel I'm going nuts.

I've had it with niblicks and tees;
Can't stand it any more.
A golfing widow? Not for me.
I'm out the nearest door.

I'll get a loan (in that man's name)
So I can cruise the globe
And find a new man of my own
Who is a golfing-phobe!

# *Close Encounters of the Household Kind*

*Part I:*
*An Unwanted Visitor*

I had a brief encounter with an eight-legged beast.
I found him in my bath on the day of Norwood's Feast.
He was sitting very quietly – not scrambling about.
But his size and shape – oh Lordy! – they just freaked me out.

I went and made a pot of tea
And drank it like a balm.
It did the trick, and very soon
My beating heart was calm.

Remembering encounters which I'd dealt with in the past,
I took my two-stage action to banish him quite fast.
I named him George, I talked to him, and told him what to do.
When he looked as though he understood, I moved on to stage two.

I went and fetched a plastic bin and brush with bristles thin.
With trembling hands I held the bin and gently brushed him in.
He reached the bottom of the bin and scrambled all about,
But the plastic sides were much too smooth for him to climb right out.

I carried him outside my door and to the garden's end,
Put the bin down and spoke to him: "Now, George, my scary friend,
You mustn't come into my house. You cause me endless stress.
Stay outside here where you belong. Long life and happiness!"

# *Close Encounters of the Household Kind*

### *Part II:*
### *Suddenly, Last Summer*

I had a brief encounter with a bluebottle one day.
He'd got in through my window and he wouldn't
   go away.
He buzzed around and dive-bombed in his panic
   to escape
And landed on the icing of my newly baked fruit cake.

He was stuck fast – oh Lordy me! – "What can I
   do?" I cried.
"Why did you choose my baking day to venture
   here inside?"
His wings beat fast as a hummingbird. He tried and
   tried to rise,
But sad to say, the end result – he was deeper in the ice.

I went and made a pot of tea
And drank it like a balm
It did the trick, and very soon
My beating heart was calm.

I fetched a spatula, my friends,
Out of the kitchen drawer.
I used it like a lever,
Till my arms were really sore.

Slowly and with utmost care
I levered him right out.
Each leg had a little icing shoe
Which blueboy set about.

He licked each leg in turn, my friends,
Till each was shining clean,
Then groomed his face, took flight at last
And never more was seen.

# *Comfort*

*(With apologies to Dr. Zeuss)*

You've got to keep your pecker up.
Be ready if it droops.
And if by chance it should fall off,
Just pick it up – say, "Whoops!"

You've got to keep your pecker up.
You've managed it before
Despite the overwhelming odds
This time recovery's sure.

You've got to keep your pecker up.
What options do you have?
Run off to Oz? Read lots of Boz?
Retreat for days to the lav?

No! Folks like you just do not flag;
They keep their peckers high.
However dark each day may be
At midnight it will die!

You've got brains in your head,
You've got feet in your shoes.
You're as strong as a lion.
You simply can't lose.

Triumph will come – believe me, I know.
Quite when I can't be precise.
But soon, very soon – the next time we meet –
You'll be feeling much more nice!

# *What a Blow!*

It was on a Tuesday morning,
Not bad for the time of year.
I had noticed dark clouds gathering west
But they weren't very near.

I pottered round the front garden,
Doing what I love most:
Weeding and deadheading,
Horticulturally engrossed!

I wondered what the shouting was,
But didn't pay attention.
Now there's a lesson for all of us
To escape fate's intervention.

The gust was such a stunner
It blew me off my feet.
Before I knew what caused it
I was halfway down our street.

I lay face down and very still,
Saw stars all circling round.
How strange – the road I was lying on
Felt soft and comfy ground.

And in a mist, I then beheld
A vision of my days.
A potted version of my life
From youth to current days.

I was a toddler dressed in white,
Tottering from side to side
In my grandma's house, where many a time
I often would reside.

I was a teenager with long black hair.
Child of the '60s, me.
The Stones and Beatles and Joan Baez,
That was the music for me.

My mum and dad, and sister too,
Appeared in vintage gear.
Then quick as a flash, I was wed and a mum;
Two kids so small and dear.

My working life transformed me:
Power suits and six-inch heels.
(No wonder my feet are now out of shape;
Hugely painful they both feel.)

I left office life and, lo and behold,
My grandchildren ran in.
My hair, dearie me, was going all grey.
I had wrinkles all over my skin.

At this point, the vision just faded.
All was dark for a long, long time.
Then I finally saw a chink of bright light;
From afar, heard a distant bell chime.

*This is the end*, I thought to myself;
*Now I will know at last*
*What lies ahead in the spirit world.*
I really felt small and aghast!

"Are you awake at last, my dear?"
A dulcet voice enquired.
"We're all so pleased to know that
You have really not expired."

I blinked three times and looked around.
White coats ringed my bed.
I frowned, sat up and cleared my throat.
"What's up, doc?" I said.

"Why am I here, and why are you here?
And why are you shedding some tears?"
"You copped a knockout blow, my dear,
And have been here for thirteen years!"

# *Mr Gloomy*

*(With apologies to W. S. Gilbert.)*

*(In November 2016, The Daily Mail dubbed Chancellor Philip Hammond as 'Mr Gloomy'.)*

Our dear Chancellor's announced his autumn recipe
To keep our country on a steady course.
He has juggled with the figures of our great economy
Which most people think has made the matter worse.

*Chorus*
When economic duty's to be done, to be done
A Chancellor's lot is not a happy one, happy one.

With the OBR producing long-term forecasts of their own
Based on chicken livers, entrails and the like.
And if their old intestines show some early signs of rot
They just raise the national debt another spike.

*Chorus*
When economic duty's to be done, to be done
A Chancellor's lot is not a happy one, happy one.

The Chancellor wants to raise the living wage an awful lot,
But the PM thinks this is a backward step.
Better to give the CBI some corp. tax relief
Hoping to give our GDP some pep!

*Chorus*
When economic duty's to be done, to be done
A Chancellor's lot is not a happy one, happy one.

It's on account of Brexit that his budget's full of gloom.
Increasingly the Leave result's the elephant in the room.
So he can't win, and we must grit our teeth and wait
Till 2019 or later brings the grim news of our fate.

*Chorus*
When economic duty's to be done, to be done
A Chancellor's lot is not a happy one, happy one.

If our Chancellor's too gloomy, how about a change?
Let's look for someone else our national finance to arrange.
Young George, our erstwhile Chancellor, is not the nation's choice,
But I think Mr Blobby would make everyone rejoice.

For he would take the national purse
And fling it far and wide,
And empty it in one great splurge;
Leave not one coin behind.
There'd be nothing for the Treasury or OBR to do
So the savings on their salaries could come to me and you.

*Chorus*
So when economic duty's to be done, to be done
Mr Blobby's lot is nothing but pure fun!

# A Modern Biblical Tale

Dear Father, this letter may not go down well
With you or dear Mother – I just cannot tell.
To hear from your son after all of this time
May cause you to weep or to curse me and mine.

I hope you will understand why I ran off.
I was bored with just working and no time off.
I took all your cards, your wallet, your cash,
And headed for freedom and a big lifelong bash.

I flung roses around and I drank to excess,
Bought all my mistresses a new dress.
Had fast cars and aeroplanes, learnt how to fly,
Took various drugs and the odd legal high.

Then Nemesis struck me; I really can't moan.
I've spent all your money and now am alone.

I'm writing to you from my horrible hovel
To say that I'm ready to meekly grovel.
To say that I'm sorry for running away
And failing to let you know I'm OK.

I'm sending this letter inside the Good Book
And where I have marked it, I'd like you to look,
And if you are willing my sins to forgive,
Can your Prodigal Son come on home now to live?

I'm hoping 'gainst hope that you'll read this and laugh
And welcome me home with a roast Fatted Calf!

# *The Training Course*

They sent us on a training course,
A residential one,
In some impersonal hotel.
Not my idea of fun!

I got there late, booked myself in,
But didn't sleep a wink.
The bed was hard, the room too hot,
The air con on the blink.

I rose at crack of dawn next day.
My head was addle-brained,
And even after breakfast
Not ready to be trained.

The subject was diversity;
The lecturer so boring
That as the morning dragged along,
I nearly fell to snoring.

And after training all the morn,
I sure had had enough.
What was the point of staying on
To hear this dreary stuff?

I signed in for the afternoon
But couldn't bear to stay.
Decided to play truant
And quietly slip away.

I skipped around the nearby town,
Had coffees by the score.
I bought myself some luxuries
From the posh local store.

I sneaked back to the crap hotel
In time for evening drinks.
Do I dare join the others
After my high jinks?

The hotel bar was crowded
*Good-oh*, I thought – *with luck*
*I may sneak in unnoticed.*
And oh so carefully I snuck.

I got myself a glass in hand
And wandered round the fringe
Of loudly chattering people.
Their talk just made me cringe.

Then as the maître d' announced
That dinner would be served,
I started feeling confident
That I'd been unobserved.

But as the crowds went off to dine,
There loomed up in my sight,
A frowning figure of a man
Who filled me with great fright.

One look at him – *Oh no, oh please
Don't let it be my boss.*
His gimlet eyes were scaring me.
I was really at a loss.

Where should I go? What should I do?
Escape was my desire.
My hand reached out as in a trance,
Pressed the red button marked *Fire*.

Everyone came running out
In mad and panicked flight,
Heading for the assembly point
Far, far into the night.

I milled around for quite a while,
As if quite mystified.
And when the all-clear was announced,
I then trooped back inside.

I joined the crowd for dinner,
Ate swiftly and then rose.
I must get up into my room,
Get changed and pack my clothes.

I got as far as the hotel lift,
Then heard a voice behind.
My heart beat fast: it was my boss.
I was in another bind.

"So there you are, Miss Jones," he said.
"I've watched you all day here.
I need to have a private word
Where no one else can hear.

"In confidence, I've been promoted
To the new Chief's post.
I'll be needing an Assistant
And would recommend you most!"

I was gobsmacked; gaped in wonder.
(Had my sins not been observed?)
Perhaps some maverick behaviour
Brings one riches undeserved!

# A Poetic Quandary

I was just wondering, as you do,
If I could pen a line or two
When the whole of my brain is blank.
No fuel left inside the tank.

I find myself at a total loss
When what I'm writing is just dross.
There must be something I can do
To let my genius come through.

I've called upon my usual muse
To find for me a cunning ruse;
Some trick to spark my inspiration
And a poetic conflagration.

I've called her once, I've called her thrice.
Had no response. Not very nice.
I've asked the others, who only say
She's over the hills and far away.

If my muse won't help and my brain won't work,
What else can I do? I mustn't shirk.
Creative writing must hold sway,
So desperate measures are the only way.

A bit of plagiarism might well do,
As long as nobody here has a clue
And happens to know the piece quite well.
Then I'm in trouble. What the hell?!

Underground, overground, wondering free,
The amateur writers of Wimbledon, we.
Making a mess of the prompt we've been given,
To a state of near madness we've been driven.

It's just no use, there's no remedy here.
Just go for the short and simple, my dear.
In these dire and troubled times,
Just have a go at five lines.

I've got to make use of 'just wondering'
And find a good rhyme without blundering.
If words I can pick
For a great limerick,
I won't need to do any plundering.

# *Lower Watha*

*(With apologies to Henry Wadsworth Longfellow.)*

In an ancient Celtic village
By the name of Lower Watha,
Stands a dwelling made of horse dung,
Fragrant-smelling, patched with grasses.
Grasses from the plains around it,
Plains where runs the flowing river,
Source of life and source of power
To protect Lower Watha's people.

At the door of that small dwelling
Stands a crone of ancient vintage.
She who, since she was a newborn,
Grew and flourished in that village.
Grew and flourished in that dwelling.
Never had she travelled from it.
Never had she left its boundary.
She who speaks to river spirits
Stays to guard those charmed waters.

As she stands outside her dwelling,
As she looks towards the river,
She begins to chant in rhythm.
Chants the words of ancient magic.
Calls upon the river spirits
For their aid in time of weeping.
Aid to stem the falling water,
Stem the flow from sky to river.

"Forty moons have passed, O Spirits!
Forty moons have seen the drenching.
They have seen the river rising,
Seen the banks begin to crumble,
Seen young trees begin to topple.
Help us, spirits, use your powers.
Stop the skies above from weeping.
We implore you, Water Spirits,
Rescue us before we perish."

At her words, the river shuddered;
Heaved its waters to a standstill.
Standstill built a mighty column;
Built it ever higher and higher.

Till it reached the skies above it,
Joined itself to skies above it,
Made a cataclysmic junction.
Split the clouds above the river,
Split apart that weeping ceiling,
Deafening all who saw and heard it,
Then fell back into the river.

All was quiet. Eerie silence
Spread across that ancient landscape.
River flowed, and rain retreated.
Mighty Sun restored its glory,
Mighty Sun gave warmth and blessings.
In that ancient Celtic village,
No more weeping skies did threaten.
Only weeping eyes replaced them.
All were mourning for their guardian.
All were mourning her lost spirit.
For their guardian crone had left them.
Given her life to bring them safety.

## Out for a Coffee etc

Would you like to go out for a coffee
And partake of a slice of banoffee?
I wouldn't be keen, nor
In Costa be seen,
So I'll just have some Harrogate toffee.

Would you like to go out for a coffee?
Or shall I go down to the offie,
And bring back brown ale
In a giant-sized pail?
That should get rid of your cough-ee!

Would you like to go out for a tea?
Just a cup, with a sandwich or three?
You can have what you like,
Then a spin on your bike.
You'll soon feel as fit as a flea!

Would you like to go out for a beer?
The local is not far from here.
We could sink several brews,
Twenty-four if you choose,
And stagger back home – you can steer.

# The Humongous Supper

That night at supper, anger was rife.
Could have cut the atmosphere with a knife.
First there was silence, then a great din
As first one or two and then all joined in.

How did it start? Who struck the first blow?
That's something that no one professes to know.
The punches and kicks came fast on that night.
No Queensbury rules had a place in this fight.

A kind of a madness had seized one and all;
Even the host and the hostess did brawl.
One thing I am really sorry to say:
The Reverend gentleman joined in the fray.

It's hard to explain why this meal went so wrong.
The daytime events had gone like a song,
With plenty of good humour and interesting talk
Between all the parties who'd been on the walk.

The walk was an annual gathering of friends
Who lived far apart in the world – at its ends.
For all but one day in every whole year,
They lived their own lives, far apart, nowhere near.

And yet with great diligence they all marked the date
Of each year's great walk – they just couldn't wait.
They planned all their journeys and where they would stay;
Looked forward with pleasure to this halcyon day.

All previous gatherings had gone really well,
Exchanging their news and their gossip as well,
And it really is strange that in this one year
A fracas had ruined their usual good cheer.

The very next day as each person departed,
With little eye contact and clearly downhearted,
In everyone's mind, the thought that was upper
Was *What on earth caused such a humongous supper?*

# Posh Poetic Footie

The sun slants peacefully upon the grass
And all is still. Then suddenly,
The calm is broken by the yelling of the mass
Of onlookers, chanting their joyous psalm.
They praise the line of noble men
In spotless garb, with faces all serene,
Quite unaware they hold not Fortune's hand.
For them, the future dim is best unseen.
Their willing feet are destined not to be
Those happy ones that guide the fateful sphere
Between those poles, and they, dismayed, will see
Their rivals' jubilance, their joy will hear.
But Fortune now seems still within their reach,
And, mocking, stretches forth her hand to each.

# *Signora Brava*

And when the old Reaper came, he came quietly and with reverence.

He left his black robes and faceless hood and scythe at home.
He came instead in the softest robes of dove grey, with shoes of feather-down that made no sound.
He looked at her with soft glances and with compassion.

He knew that, while he had waited for her in the wings, she had played out the last season of her life with a bravura performance – hiding the pain and the bewilderment behind an ever-smiling face; ever conscious of the feelings of those she loved and who loved her.

And when the final curtain came, he glided gently to her side. He looked down at her tenderly and, stretching out his hands, drew forth her spirit from its earthly home. He cradled her in the soft folds of his robes and rose into the great, endless plains of the skies, far beyond the reach of skylarks.

He knew the pathway to the hidden gate of that other world which no earth-living being can discover. With kind and gentle words, he set her free – free to become another being in a way of life that none of us can know until we too follow her into the yonder.

# Spring Flowers at War

In the springtime of the year,
In my garden of which I'm so proud,
I wandered among the beauteous blooms
And spoke my thoughts out loud.

"Thank you for blooming first in the spring.
You're wondrous beyond all telling.
You daffs and tulips and crocuses
And anemone blandas (check spelling)."

"Excuse me." There came a piping voice.
"Excuse me just for a minute.
I am the earliest to push through the earth;
Those bulbs that you name are still in it.

"I battle my way to the surface each year
Though I'm but a dainty wee thing.
My beauty and colour – a virginal white –
The very essence of spring.

"Surely the Snowdrop must take pride of place
As the true herald of Spring.
Those others you've named are way down the list
It's me that should be crowned King."

A daff then responded in petulant tones,
"You're too small to claim pride of place.
You're so often hidden beneath trees and shrubs
Where nobody sees your face.

"My height and bright colours have impact and flair;
They light up dark days all around.
I flourish my trumpet and flutter my leaves;
Your miniscule bell makes no sound."

"Hang on a minute," the crocus cried.
"You two don't have the sole claim
To being spring's harbinger. Others like me
Have the right to make such a claim.

"I'm small and dainty, but in my case
Can be yellow or purple or white.
This palette of colours you two do not have;
You cannot create such a sight."

"And what about me?" the aconite yelled.
"Just 'cause I grow in wild spaces,
It doesn't detract from my candidature
As earliest bird in these races."

As this war of words reached unbearable volume,
Old Adam the gardener appeared.
"Enough of this quarrelling!
It is not allowed. The penalty is to be feared!"

The bulbs stopped their shouting and, silence regained,
They waited their fate with trepidation.
But Old Adam spoke in a quiet voice:
"What you need is some fresh education.

"In the great Scheme when the world began,
The Architect drew up a master plan.
A plan that would pleasure the race of men,
For whom he had made it as only he can.

"Now what you've forgotten is that each one of you,
Of particular species and shape and hue,
Has your role to play in the overall Scheme.
Each flower is special and needs to be seen.

"So keep yourself strong. Play your own special part
By blooming in season – a true work of art.
Then sleep, store your goodness to make quite sure
That next spring will show off its glory once more."

# *Detritus*

You see them everywhere these days,
Wherever you may roam.
You step outside your door each day;
They lurk there by your home.

They clutter up the pavements,
Make local parks a mess,
Those little cardboard boxes
That I for one detest.

They travel far when sharp winds blow,
And wilt in showers of rain.
Our city is awash with them.
They really are a pain.

Where do they come from, and what for?
And are they such a curse?
Surely the doggy doo-doos
That do more harm are worse?

They're chicken-and-chips containers
Once full of salt and grease.
Our schoolkids' staple diet!
No wonder they're all obese!

# *Holiday Rap*

The best of holidays, from my point of view,
Are the ones when you're small and holidays are new.

For months in advance the grown-ups are talking.
They say I'll enjoy it when they take me walking.

They chatter on and on about places we'll see.
Not a single place name is known to me.

There's talk of the sea and the lovely seashore,
How I'll swim in the ocean and ask for more.

I'll ride on a donkey across the sand.
They say that the feeling of riding is grand.

They tell me we'll see a magical show
With Punch and with Judy with a baby in tow.

I quite like the sound of it, tho' there's a croc
Who might jump out and eat me from behind a rock.

And talking of rock, it's a lovely pink stick
That makes you quite sticky and makes you feel sick.

I know that my mum will really be cross
When I'm entirely covered in pink candyfloss.

But one of the seaside things I'll enjoy
Is eating fish and chips – it's the real McCoy.

They'll give me some coins to play the arcade.
It's gone in just two minutes – no profit's been made.

But Mum'll get excited when she wins a prize
On the bingo stall. It's not very nice.

It's a lurid dog that's made of chalk.
I drop it on the pavement when we go for a walk.

And when the day is over they'll carry me back
To the little old caravan – quite a shack.

There are two thin beds and not one more
Mum and Dad can't sleep together or they'll fall on
   the floor.

That just leaves me – and tired as I am,
I could really sleep most anywhere – or just in my pram.

Oh, the joys of a holiday you've never had before.
There's nothing to beat them – so give me more!

## Corn Circles

Runic marks on the English landscape.
Cuneiform channels scored in the grass.
Could it be visitors from deepest space-lands,
Marking out territory as they pass?

All those marks and all those channels
Mystify the human race.
The meaning of those shapes and figures
Quite impossible to trace.

Some people claim the fairy folk,
Or perhaps the Great God Pan,
May have left those symbols
Long before our world began.

If that be true, then they will last
As long as Time holds sway.
And only vanish if this fair Earth
Declares, "Time's up!" one day.

# The Pillage of London

Is there a law against stealing the sky?
For stealing the joy of a crisp winter's day when the
 snow clouds foregather in all shades of grey?
For stealing the rush of a mad March day as clouds
 scud so fast when the wild wind's at play?
For stealing the peace of a summer blue sky with
 fluffy white clouds that gracefully fly?

The planners and architects seeking renown
Have stolen the sky in old London town.
Who gave them permission
To hide from our view
The cotton-wool clouds
And cerulean blue?
Even the best of a bright summer's day
Reduced to a sliver – all but gone away.
London is now such an ugly place
Diminished, of beauty bereft
Architects, planners, money-grabbers and builders
Have spoiled what her history left.
The dear ancient buildings
Which do still survive

Are surrounded and dwarfed by
The huge swamping tide
Of brutalist towers of steelwork and glass
With no trace of embellishment, no touch of class.
They tower from pavements, breathtakingly high,
They loom terrifyingly on those who pass by
Who, when they look up, their hearts sink and cry,
*Who let them steal our most beautiful sky?*